Olimpia
Easy y
Ens

The Lady That's
Known as Lou

(An Actor Celebrates Robert Service)

Clint Ward

Copyright Notice

This work is available through Spitfire Productions. For information about stage performance rights or to order scripts, please contact: 416 884 4762

Design by Stephen Walters, Oxygen Publishing
Edited by Terry O'Shaughnessy
Illustrations used in this book are © CBC/Bob Binks

Email: clintward@videotron.ca
Website: www.clintward.ca

ISBN: 9798555522801
Imprint: Independently published

Dedicated to Airlie McPhee
who puts up with my many hours
of dreaming and writing.

Empty Spaces

We live in challenging times with our theatres closed and the cinema beam of light turned off. I saw an interesting quote recently flashing on my phone with great insistence –

This is not a year to get everything we want.

This is the year to appreciate everything we have.

Good theatre and stimulating film are a memory at the moment, It might be a good time to appreciate the great entertainments of the past when reading the poems of Robert Service gave us the stimulation we craved on long winter nights. It would be a simple matter to bring forth his 'writings for the people' again. An actor of feeling and talent could illuminate the poems and it would be a good evening of fun and laughter which is just what we need. Turn on the lights and watch a single actor, distanced as needed by the times, bring Robert Service to life again. Enjoy.

Clint Ward, (November, 2020)

The Lady That's Known as Lou
(An Actor Celebrates Robert Service)
By
Clint Ward

This is a play to be delivered by one actor. It is a possibly simple set, a literary space, with a desk, some shelves with books and a comfortable chair for reading. A wooden reading stand. The actor needs to comfortably use the space so the performance is not static. Decisions on how to design the set are up to the director and the actor. It is, in effect, a one-man or one-woman show. Verses from the many volumes of Service's poetry can be added or deleted.

Actor:

I have no doubt the Devil grins,
As seas of ink I spatter
Ye Gods forget my literary sins
The other kind don't matter

A September 16, 1958 newspaper obituary about the passing of a great Canadian poet who died at his home in Lancieux, France at the age of 84 reads as follows:

'He was not a poet's poet. Fancy-Dan dilettantes will dispute the description "great." He was a people's poet. To the people he was great. They understood him, and knew that any verse carrying the by-line of Robert W. Service would be a lilting thing, clear, clean and power-packed, beating out a story with a dramatic intensity that made the nerves tingle. And he was no poor, garret-type poet, either. His stuff made money hand over fist. One piece alone, *The Shooting of Dan McGrew*, rolled up half a million dollars for him.'

Ah yes, I know my brow is low
And often wished it high.
So that I might with rapture write
An epic of the sky;

A poem cast in contour vast;
Of fabled gods and fays;
A classic screed that few would read
Yet nearly all would praise.

******

So come, good men who toil and tire,
Who smoke and sip the kindly cup.
Ring round about the tavern fire
Ere yet you drink your liquor up;
And hear my simple songs of earth,
Of youth and truth and living things;
Of poverty and proper mirth.
Of rags and rich imaginings;
Of cock-a-hoop, blue-heavened days,
Of hearts elate and eager breath,
Of wonder, worship, pity, praise,

Of sorrow, sacrifice and death;
Of lusting laughter, passion, pain,
Of lights that lure and dreams that thrall
And if golden word I gain,
Oh, kindly folks, God save you all!
And if you shake your heads in blame
Good friends, God love you all the same.

"The only society I like," he once said, "is that which is rough and tough - and the tougher the better. That's where you get down to bedrock and meet human people." He found that kind of society in the Yukon gold rush, and he immortalized it.

The lonely sunsets flare forlorn
Down valleys dreadly desolate;
The lordly mountains soar in scorn
As still as death, as stern as fate.

The lonely sunsets flame and die;
The giant valleys gulp the night;
The Monster Mountains scrape the sky,
Where eager stars are diamond-bright.

So gaunt against the gibbous moon,
Piercing the silence velvet-piled,
A lone wolf howls his ancient rune --
The fell arch-spirit of the Wild.

Robert W. Service was best known for his rollicking, robust poems of the gold rush days in the Klondike and many were written quickly. He listened intently to the gold rush yarns that Dawson mining men often talked about in the bars. One such tale was about a fellow who cremated his pal. After hearing this, Service spent the night walking in the woods composing a poem which he wrote down from memory the next day. This narrative is about the responsibility of a promise given.

There are strange things done in the midnight sun
By the men who moil for gold;
The Arctic trails have their secret tales
That would make your blood run cold;
The Northern Lights have seen queer sights,
But the queerest they ever did see
Was that night on the marge of Lake Lebarge
I cremated Sam McGee.

Now Sam McGee was from Tennessee,
Where the cotton blooms and blows.
Why he left his home in the South to roam
'Round the Pole, God only knows.
He was always cold, but the land of gold
Seemed to hold him like a spell;
Though he'd often say in his homely way
That he'd "sooner live in hell".

On a Christmas Day we were mushing our way
Over the Dawson trail.
Talk of your cold! Through the parka's fold
It stabbed like a driven nail.

If our eyes we'd close, then the lashes froze
Till sometimes we couldn't see;
It wasn't much fun, but the only one
To whimper was Sam McGee.

And that very night, as we lay packed tight
In our robes beneath the snow,
And the dogs were fed, and the stars o'erhead
Were dancing heel and toe,
He turned to me, and "Cap," says he,
"I'll cash in this trip, I guess;
And if I do, I'm asking that you
Won't refuse my last request."

Well, he seemed so low that I couldn't say no;
Then he says with a sort of moan:
"It's the cursed cold, and it's got right hold
Till I'm chilled clean through to the bone.
Yet 'tain't being dead -- it's my awful dread
Of the icy grave that pains;
So I want you to swear that, foul or fair,
You'll cremate my last remains."

A pal's last need is a thing to heed,
So I swore I would not fail;
And we started on at the streak of dawn;
But God! he looked ghastly pale.
He crouched on the sleigh, and he raved all day
Of his home in Tennessee;
And before nightfall a corpse was all
That was left of Sam McGee.

There wasn't a breath in that land of death,
And I hurried, horror-driven,
With a corpse half hid that I couldn't get rid,
Because of a promise given;
It was lashed to the sleigh, and it seemed to say:
"You may tax your brawn and brains,
But you promised true, and it's up to you
To cremate those last remains."

Now a promise made is a debt unpaid,
And the trail has its own stern code.
In the days to come, though my lips were dumb,
In my heart how I cursed that load.
In the long, long night, by the lone firelight,
While the huskies, round in a ring,
Howled out their woes to the homeless snows
O God! how I loathed the thing.

And every day that quiet clay
Seemed to heavy and heavier grow;
And on I went, though the dogs were spent
And the grub was getting low;
The trail was bad, and I felt half mad,
But I swore I would not give in;
And I'd often sing to the hateful thing,
And it hearkened with a grin.

Till I came to the marge of Lake Lebarge,
And a derelict there lay;
It was jammed in the ice, but I saw in a trice
It was called the "Alice May".
And I looked at it, and I thought a bit,

And I looked at my frozen chum;
Then "Here," said I, with a sudden cry,
"Is my cre-ma-tor-eum."

Some planks I tore from the cabin floor,
And I lit the boiler fire;
Some coal I found that was lying around,
And I heaped the fuel higher;
The flames just soared, and the furnace roared
Such a blaze you seldom see;
And I burrowed a hole in the glowing coal,
And I stuffed in Sam McGee.

Then I made a hike, for I didn't like
To hear him sizzle so;
And the heavens scowled,
and the huskies howled,
And the wind began to blow.
It was icy cold, but the hot sweat
rolled down my cheeks,
and I don't know why;
And the greasy smoke in an inky cloak
Went streaking down the sky.

I do not know how long in the snow
I wrestled with grisly fear;
But the stars came out and they danced about
Ere again I ventured near;
I was sick with dread, but I bravely said:
"I'll just take a peep inside.
I guess he's cooked, and it's time I
looked"; . . . Then the door I opened wide.

And there sat Sam, looking cool and calm,
In the heart of the furnace roar;
And he wore a smile you could see a mile,
And he said: "Please close that door.
It's fine in here, but I greatly fear
You'll let in the cold and storm
Since I left Plumtree, down in Tennessee,
It's the first time I've been warm."

There are strange things done in the midnight sun
By the men who moil for gold;
The Arctic trails have their secret tales
That would make your blood run cold;
The Northern Lights have seen queer sights,
But the queerest they ever did see
Was that night on the marge of Lake Lebarge
I cremated Sam McGee.

Service claimed that many of his Yukon poems were written from sheer boredom with the endless repetition of popular ballads by Rudyard Kipling and the American standbys, *Casey at the Bat* and *The Face on the Ballroom Floor*, all features of the concerts that were the main form of public entertainment during his Whitehorse days working in a bank. He did not recite his own poems but instead threw them in a drawer until enough had accumulated and he thought it might be possible to bind them together in a booklet - which he could give to his friends. He found a publisher and in 1907, *Songs of a Sourdough*, with its melodramatic situations, rollicking rhythms and rough-neck vocabulary became an immediate success.

The waves have a story to tell me,
As I lie on the lonely beach;
Chanting aloft in the pine-tops,
The wind has a lesson to teach;
But the stars sing an anthem of glory
I cannot put into speech.

The waves tell of ocean spaces,
Of hearts that are wild and brave,
Of populous city places,
Of desolate shores they lave,
Of men who sally in quest of gold
To sink in an ocean grave.

The wind is a mighty roamer;
He bids me keep me free,
Clean from the taint of the gold-lust,
Hardy and pure as he;
Cling with my love to nature,
As a child to the mother-knee.

But the stars throng out in their glory,
And they sing of the God in man;
They sing of the Mighty Master,
Of the loom his fingers span,
Where a star or a soul
is a part of the whole,
And weft in the wondrous plan.

Here by the camp-fire's flicker,
Deep in my blanket curled,
I long for the peace of the pine-gloom,

When the scroll of the Lord is unfurled,
And the wind and the wave are silent,
And world is singing to world.

******

The Dreamer visioned Life as it might be,
And from his dream forthright a picture grew,
A painting all the people thronged to see,
And joyed therein –

Till came the Man Who Knew, Saying: "'Tis bad!
Why do ye gape, ye fools!
He painteth not according to the schools."

The Dreamer probed Life's mystery of woe,
And in a book he sought to give the clue;
The people read, and saw that it was so,
And read again.

Then came the Man Who Knew, Saying:
"Ye witless ones! this book is vile:
He hath not got the rudiments of style."

Love smote the Dreamer's lips, and silver clear
He sang a song so sweet, so tender true,
That all the market-place was thrilled to hear,
And listened rapt –

Till came the Man Who Knew,

Saying: "His technique's wrong; he singeth ill.
Waist not your time."

The singer's voice was still.
And then the people roused as if from sleep,
Crying: "What care we if it be not Art!

Hath he not charmed us, made us laugh and weep?
Come, let us crown him where he sits apart."
Then with his picture spurned,
His book unread, His song unsung,
They found their Dreamer – dead.

****

My Father Christmas passed away
When I was barely seven.
At twenty one, alack-a-day,
I lost my hope of Heaven.

Yet not in either lies the curse:
The hell of it's because
I don't know which loss hurt the worse –
My God or Santa Claus.

Songs of a Sourdough was reprinted in 1908 as *The Spell of
the Yukon* and it made Robert Service wealthy. In 1909, the
bank he worked for in Whitehorse wanted him to become
manager—and it was a pretty good promotion. But the

call of the rhyme, and the new-found dollars that passion brought him, could not be denied. He decided to resign and that was the end of the banking business.

He rented a small two-room cabin on Eighth Avenue in Dawson City and began his career as a full-time author by starting to work on a novel. Service went for walks that lasted all night, slept till mid-afternoon, and sometimes didn't come out of the cabin for days. In five months the novel, *The Trail of '98*, was complete and he took it to a publisher in New York where it became an immediate best-seller.

In 1912, Service left Canada and went to France where he served as a reporter for *The Toronto Star* during the Balkan War of 1912-1913.

Now Kelly was no fighter;
He loved his pipe and glass;
An easygoing blighter,
Who lived in Montparnasse.
But 'mid the tavern tattle
He heard some guinney say:
"When France goes forth to battle,
The Legion leads the way.

"The scourings of creation,
Of every sin and station,
The men who've known damnation,
Are picked to lead the way."

Well, Kelly joined the Legion;
They marched him day and night;
They rushed him to the region
Where largest loomed the fight.
"Behold your mighty mission,
Your destiny," said they;
"By glorious tradition
The Legion leads the way.

"With tattered banners flying
With trail of dead and dying,
On! On! All hell defying,
The Legion sweeps the way."

With grim, hard-bitten faces,
With jests of savage mirth,
They swept into their places,
The men of iron worth;
Their blooded steel was flashing;
They swung to face the fray;
Then rushing, roaring, crashing,
The Legion cleared the way.

The trail they blazed was gory;
Few lived to tell the story;
Through death they plunged to glory;
But, oh, they cleared the way.

Now Kelly lay a-dying,
And dimly saw advance,
With split new banners flying,
The fantassins of France.

Then up amid the mêlée
He rose from where he lay;
"Come on, me boys," says Kelly,
"The Layjun lades the way!"

Aye, while they faltered, doubting
(Such flames of doom were spouting),
He caught them, thrilled them, shouting:
"The Layjun lades the way!"

They saw him slip and stumble,
Then stagger on once more;
They marked him trip and tumble,
A mass of grime and gore;
They watched him blindly crawling
Amid hell's own affray,
And calling, calling, calling:
"The Layjun lades the way!"

And even while they wondered,
The battle-wrack was sundered;
To victory they thundered,
But . . . Kelly led the way.

Still Kelly kept a-going;
Beserker-like he ran;
His eyes with fury glowing,
A lion of a man;
His rifle madly swinging,
His soul athirst to slay,
His slogan ringing, ringing,
"The Layjun lades the way!"

Till in a pit death-baited,
Where Huns with Maxims waited,
He plunged . . . and there blood-sated,
To death he stabbed his way.

Now Kelly was a fellow
Who simply loathed a fight;
He loved a tavern mellow,
Grog hot and pipe alight;
I'm sure the Show appalled him,
And yet without dismay,
When death and duty called him,
He up and led the way.

So in Valhalla drinking
(If heroes meek and shrinking
Are suffered there), I'm thinking
'Tis Kelly leads the way.

France seemed to be a welcome place to live and Service settled in Paris, living in the Latin Quarter. In June of 1913 he married Germaine Bourgoin and they purchased a summer home at Lancieux, Côtes-d'Armor, in Brittany.

He was 41 when World War I broke out and he briefly covered the war for the *Toronto Star*. He also worked as a stretcher bearer and ambulance driver with the American Red Cross, until his health broke.

In 1916, another book of poetry was published, *Rhymes of a Red Cross Man*. The book was dedicated to the memory of his brother, Lieutenant Albert Service, Canadian Infantry, Killed in Action, France, August 1916.

I'm dead.
Officially I'm dead. Their hope is past.
How long I stood as missing! Now, at last I'm dead
Look in my face -- no likeness can you see,
No tiny trace of him they knew as "me".
How terrible the change!
Even my eyes are strange.
So keyed are they to pain,
That if I chanced to meet
My mother in the street
She'd look at me in vain.

When she got home I think she'd say:
"I saw the saddest sight to-day --
A poilu with no face at all.
Far better in the fight to fall
Than go through life like that, I think.
Poor fellow! how he made me shrink.
No face. Just eyes that seemed to stare
At me with anguish and despair.
This ghastly war! I'm almost cheered
To think my son who disappeared,
My boy so handsome and so gay,
Might have come home like him to-day."

I'm dead. I think it's better to be dead
When little children look at you with dread;
And when you know you're coming home again
Will only give the ones who love you pain.
Ah! who can help but shrink? One cannot blame.
They see the hideous husk, not, not the flame
Of sacrifice and love that burns within;

While souls of satyrs, riddled through with sin,
Have bodies fair and excellent to see.
Mon Dieu! how different we all would be
If this our flesh was ordained to express
Our spirit's beauty or its ugliness.

Oh, you who look at me with fear to-day,
And shrink despite yourselves, and turn away --
It was for you I suffered woe accurst;
For you I braved red battle at its worst;
For you I fought and bled and maimed and slew;
For you, for you!
For you I faced hell-fury and despair;
The reeking horror of it all I knew:
I flung myself into the furnace there;
I faced the flame that scorched me with its glare;
I drank unto the dregs the devil's brew --
Look at me now -- for you and you and you. . . .

I'm thinking of the time we said good-by:
We took our dinner in Duval's that night,
Just little Jacqueline, Lucette and I;
We tried our very utmost to be bright.
We laughed. And yet our eyes, they weren't gay.
I sought all kinds of cheering things to say.
"Don't grieve," I told them. "Soon the time will pass;
My next permission will come quickly round;
We'll all meet at the Gare du Montparnasse;
Three times I've come already, safe and sound."
(But oh, I thought, it's harder every time,
After a home that seems like Paradise,
To go back to the vermin and the slime,

The weariness, the want, the sacrifice.
"Pray God," I said, "the war may soon be done,
But no, oh never, never till we've won!")

Then to the station quietly we walked;
I had my rifle and my haversack,
My heavy boots, my blankets on my back;
And though it hurt us, cheerfully we talked.
We chatted bravely at the platform gate.
I watched the clock. My train must go at eight.
One minute to the hour . . . we kissed good-by,
Then, oh, they both broke down, with piteous cry.
I went. . . . Their way was barred; they could not pass.
I looked back as the train began to start;
Once more I ran with anguish at my heart
And through the bars I kissed my little lass. . . .

Three years have gone; they've waited day by day.
I never came. I did not even write.
For when I saw my face was such a sight
I thought that I had better . . . stay away.
And so I took the name of one who died,
A friendless friend who perished by my side.
In Prussian prison camps three years of hell
I kept my secret; oh, I kept it well!
And now I'm free, but none shall ever know;
They think I died out there . . . it's better so.

To-day I passed my wife in widow's weeds.
I brushed her arm. She did not even look.
So white, so pinched her face, my heart still bleeds,
And at the touch of her, oh, how I shook!

And then last night I passed the window where
They sat together; I could see them clear,
The lamplight softly gleaming on their hair,
And all the room so full of cozy cheer.
My wife was sewing, while my daughter read;
I even saw my portrait on the wall.
I wanted to rush in, to tell them all;
And then I cursed myself: "You're dead, you're dead!"
God! how I watched them from the darkness there,
Clutching the dripping branches of a tree,
Peering as close as ever I might dare,
And sobbing, sobbing, oh, so bitterly!

But no, it's folly; and I mustn't stay.
To-morrow I am going far away.
I'll find a ship and sail before the mast;
In some wild land I'll bury all the past.
I'll live on lonely shores and there forget,
Or tell myself that there has never been
The gay and tender courage of Lucette,
The little loving arms of Jacqueline.

A man lonely upon a lonely isle,
Sometimes I'll look towards the North and smile
To think they're happy, and they both believe
I died for France, and that I lie at rest;
And for my glory's sake they've ceased to grieve,
And hold my memory sacred. Ah! that's best.
And in that thought I'll find my joy and peace
As there alone I wait the Last Release.

With the end of the war, Service settled down to being a rich man in Paris. He was reputedly the wealthiest author living in the city, yet was known to dress as a workingman and walk the streets, blending in and observing everything around him. These experiences would be used in his next book of poetry.

Ballads of a Bohemian was published in 1921, the same year that Ernest Hemingway arrived in Paris, but the two authors never met. Service was fond of saying, "I write of the things of today for the people of today." He considered himself a common poet for the common man.

> The sunshine seeks my little room
> To tell me Paris streets are gay;
> That children cry the lily bloom
> All up and down the leafy way;
> That half the town is mad with May,
> With flame of flag and boom of bell:
> For Carnival is King to-day;
> So pen and page, awhile farewell.

****

> The Rector met a little lass
> Who led a heifer by a rope.
> Said he: "Why don't you go to Mass?
> Do you not want to please the Pope?"

The village maiden made reply,
As on the rope she ceased to pull:
"My father said this morning
I must take Paquerette to see the bull."

The Rector frowned. "Tis wrong, I wist
To leave your prayer-book on the shelf.
Your father has a stronger wrist;
Why can't he do the job himself?"

Then lovely in her innocence,
With gaze as pure as meadow pool,
The maid spoke in her sire's defense:
"But Daddy, please your Reverence,
Would rather leave it to the bull."

******

She was a Philistine spick and span,
He was a bold Bohemian.
She had the mode, and the last at that;
He had a cape and a brigand hat.
She was so riant and chic and trim;
He was so shaggy, unkempt and grim.
On the rue de la Paix she was wont to shine;
The rue de la Gaîté was more his line.
She doted on Barclay and Dell and Caine;
He quoted Mallarmé and Paul Verlaine.
She was a triumph at Tango teas;
At Vorticist's suppers he sought to please.

She thought that Franz Lehar was utterly great;
Of Strauss and Stravinsky he'd piously prate.
She loved elegance, he loved art;
They were as wide as the poles apart:
Yet -- Cupid and Caprice are hand and glove --
They met at a dinner, they fell in love.

Home he went to his garret bare,
Thrilling with rapture, hope, despair.
Swift he gazed in his looking-glass,
Made a grimace and murmured: "Ass!"
Seized his scissors and fiercely sheared,
Severed his buccaneering beard;
Grabbed his hair, and clip! clip! clip!
Off came a bunch with every snip.
Ran to a tailor's in startled state,
Suits a dozen commanded straight;
Coats and overcoats, pants in pairs,
Everything that a dandy wears;
Socks and collars, and shoes and ties,
Everything that a dandy buys.
Chums looked at him with wondering stare,
Fancied they'd seen him before somewhere;
A Brummell, a D'Orsay, a beau so fine,
A shining, immaculate Philistine.

Home she went in a raptured daze,
Looked in a mirror with startled gaze,
Didn't seem to be pleased at all;
Savagely muttered: "Insipid Doll!"
Clutched her hair and a pair of shears,
Cropped and bobbed it behind the ears;

Aimed at a wan and willowy-necked
Sort of a Holman Hunt effect;
Robed in subtile and sage-green tones,
Like the dames of Rossetti and E. Burne-Jones;
Girdled her garments billowing wide,
Moved with an undulating glide;
All her frivolous friends forsook,
Cultivated a soulful look;
Gushed in a voice with a creamy throb
Over some weirdly Futurist daub --
Did all, in short, that a woman can
To be a consummate Bohemian.

A year went past with its hopes and fears,
A year that seemed like a dozen years.
They met once more. . . . Oh, at last! At last!
They rushed together, they stopped aghast.
They looked at each other with blank dismay,
They simply hadn't a word to say.
He thought with a shiver: "Can this be she?"
She thought with a shudder: "This can't be he?"
This simpering dandy, so sleek and spruce;
This languorous lily in garments loose;
They sought to brace from the awful shock:
Taking a seat, they tried to talk.
She spoke of Bergson and Pater's prose,
He prattled of dances and ragtime shows;
She purred of pictures, Matisse, Cezanne,
His tastes to the girls of Kirchner ran;
She raved of Tchaikovsky and Caesar Franck,
He owned that he was a jazz-band crank!
They made no headway. Alas! alas!

He thought her a bore, she thought him an ass.
And so they arose and hurriedly fled;
Perish Illusion, Romance, you're dead.
He loved elegance, she loved art,
Better at once to part, to part.

And what is the moral of all this rot?
Don't try to be what you know you're not.
And if you're made on a muttonish plan,
Don't seek to seem a Bohemian;
And if to the goats your feet incline,
Don't try to pass for a Philistine.

******

"Why did the lady in the lift
Slap that poor parson's face?"
Said Mother, thinking as she sniffed,
Of clerical disgrace.

Said Sonny Boy: "Alas, I know.
My conscience doth accuse me;
The lady stood upon my toe,
Yet did not say-"Excuse me!"

She hurt-and in that crowd confined
I scarcely could endure it;
So when I pinched her fat behind
She thought-it was the Curate."

******

A little child was sitting Up on her mother's knee
And down down her cheeks the bitter tears did flow.
And as I sadly listened I heard this tender plea,
'Twas uttered in a voice so soft and low.

"Not guilty" said the Jury And the Judge said "Set her free,
But remember it must not occur again.
And next time you must listen to you little daughter's plea,"
Then all the Court did join in this refrain.

Chorus:
"Please Mother don't stab Father with the BREAD-KNIFE,
Remember 'twas a gift when you were wed.
But if you must stab Father with the BREAD-KNIFE,
Please Mother use another for the BREAD."

******

When I was with a Shakespeare show
I played the part of Guildenstern,
Or Rosenkrantz-at least I know
It wasn't difficult to learn;
By Reader, do not at me scoff,
For futhermore I should explain
I was the understudy of
The understudy of the Dane.

Oh how it crabbed me just to think
They barred me from that role divine;
And how I longed to have them drink
A cup of slightly poisoned wine!
At every night with struts and rants
I strove my quid a week to earn,
And put my soul in Rosenkrantz-
Or was it haply, Guildenstern.

Alas! I might have spared by breath,
I never played the noble Dane;
And yet when Irving staged Macbeth
I bore a tree of Dunsinane,
And yearned for that barn-storming day,
Of hopes and dreams and patchy pants,
When Guildenstern I'd proudly play-
Or was, it maybe, Rosenkrantz?

******

Said the Door: "She came in
With no shadow of sin;
Turned the key in the lock,
Slipped out of her frock,
The robe she liked best
When for supper she dressed.
Then a letter she tore . . .
What a wan look she wore!"
Said the Door.

Said the Chair: "She sat down
With a pitiful frown,
And then (oh, it's queer)
Just one lonely tear
Rolled down her pale cheek.
How I hoped she would speak
As she let down her hair,"
Said the Chair.

Said the Glass: "Then she gazed
Into me like one dazed;
As with delicate grace
She made up her face,
Her cheeks and her lips
With rose finger-tips,
So lovely - alas!
Then she turned on the gas."
Said the Glass.

Said the Bed: "Down she lay
In a weariful way,
Like an innocent child,
To her fate reconciled;
Hands clasped to her breast,
In prayer or in rest:
'Dear Mother,' she said,
Then pillowed her head,"
Said the Bed.

Said the Room: "Then the gleam
Of the moon like a dream,

Soft silvered my space,
And it fell on her face
That was never so sweet
As her heart ceased to beat . . .
Then the moon fled and gloom
Fell like funeral plume,"
Said the Room.

"Just a whore,"
Said the Door;
"Yet so fair,"
Said the Chair;
"Frail, alas!"
Said the Glass;
"Now she's gone,"
Said the Bed;
"Sorry doom,"
Said the Room

Then they all,
Floor and wall,
Quiet grew,
Ceiling too;
Like a tomb
Was the room;
With hushed breath
Hailing Death:
Soul's release,
Silence, Peace.

In 1940, Service left France only a few days ahead of the advancing German troops. It was a fortunate escape because they might have been on the lookout for the poet who had written a comedic stanza or two about Hitler for a local newspaper. He returned to Canada for a time and then went to Hollywood. While there he was invited by the director of the film, *The Spoilers,* to make a cameo appearance in the film. It was a very short scene as himself having just finished his most famous work, *The Shooting of Dan McGrew.* The few short lines were with the film's star Marlene Dietrich and he found her voice so distracting that it took 17 takes to get the few lines right. The film was noted for its four minute ending scene about a bar room brawl featuring the other two stars.

Johnny Wayne and Randy Scott
They fought and fought and fought and fought
With joy they shed each other's gore,
And then they paused and shed some more.
To bust each other's blocks they strove.
They wrecked the bar and crashed the stove.
Then with a heave big Johnny Wayne
Hurled Randy through the window pane.
So in the street and down the lot
They fought and fought and fought and fought.
So fierce they mixed it up I'll bet
Them galoots might be fighting yet.

His days of the long narrative poem were gone, but he still wrote with simplicity and the ring of truth.

There's a race of men that don't fit in,
A race that can't stay still;
So they break the hearts of kith and kin,
And they roam the world at will.
They range the field and they rove the flood,
And they climb the mountain's crest;
Theirs is the curse of the gypsy blood,
And they don't know how to rest.

If they just went straight they might go far;
They are strong and brave and true;
But they're always tired of the things that are,
And they want the strange and new.
They say: "Could I find my proper groove,
What a deep mark I would make!"
So they chop and change, and each fresh move
Is only a fresh mistake.

And each forgets, as he strips and runs
With a brilliant, fitful pace,
It's the steady, quiet, plodding ones
Who win in the lifelong race.
And each forgets that his youth has fled,
Forgets that his prime is past,
Till he stands one day, with a hope that's dead,
In the glare of the truth at last.

He has failed, he has failed; he has missed his chance;
He has just done things by half.
Life's been a jolly good joke on him,
And now is the time to laugh.
Ha, ha! He is one of the Legion Lost;
He was never meant to win;
He's a rolling stone, and it's bred in the bone;
He's a man who won't fit in.

******

I haled me a woman from the street,
Shameless, but, oh so fair!
I bade her sit in the model's seat
And I painted her sitting there.

I hid all trace of her heart unclean;
I painted a babe at her breast;
I painted her as she might have been
If the Worst had been the Best.

She laughed at my picture and went away.
Then came, with a knowing nod,
A connoisseur, and I heard him say;
" 'Tis Mary, the Mother of God."

So I painted a halo round her hair,
And I sold her and took my fee,
And she hangs in the church of Saint Hillarie,
Where you and all may see.

******

Oh darling Eric, why did you
For my fond affection sue,
And then with surgeons artful aid
Transform yourself into a maid?
So now in petticoats you go
And people call you Erico.

Sometimes I wonder if they can
Change me in turn into a man;
Then after all we might get wed
And frolic on a feather bed:
Although I do not see how we
Could ever have a family.

Oh dear! Oh dear! It's so complex.
Why must they meddle with our sex.
My Eric was a handsome 'he,'
But now he--oh excuse me--she
Informs me that I must forget
I was his blond Elizabet.

Alas! These scientists of Sweden
I curse, who've robbed me of my Eden;
Who with their weird hormones inhuman
Can make a man into a woman.
Alas, poor Eric! . . . Erico
I wish you were in Jerico.

******

He asked the lady in the train
If he might smoke: she smiled consent.
So lighting his cigar and fain
To talk he puffed away content,
Reflecting: how delightful are
Fair dame and fine cigar.

Then from his bulging wallet he
A photograph with pride displayed,
His charming wife and children three,
When suddenly he was dismayed
To hear her say: "These notes you've got,--
I want the lot."

He scarcely could believe his ears.
He laughed: "The money isn't mine.
To pay it back would take me years,
And so politely I decline.
Madame, I think you speak in fun:
Have you a gun?"

She smiled. "No weapon have I got,
Only my virtue, but I swear
If you don't hand me out the lot
I'll rip my blouse, let down my hair,
Denounce you as a fiend accurst"
He told her: "Do your worst."

She did. Her silken gown she tore,
Let down her locks and pulled the cord
That stopped the train, and from the floor
She greeted engineer and guard:

"I fought and fought in vain," she cried.
"Save me,--I'm terrified!"

The man was calm; he stood aloof.
Said he: "Her game you understand;
But if you doubt, behold the proof
Of innocence is in my hand."
And as they stared into the car
They saw his logic in a flash
Aloft he held a lit cigar
With two inches of ash.

******

When Aunt Jane died we hunted round,
And money everywhere we found.
How much I do not care to say,
But no death duties will we pay,
And Aunt Jane will be well content
We bilked the bloody Government.

While others spent she loved to save,
But couldn't take it to her grave.
While others save we love to spend;
She hated us but in the end
Because she left no Testament
To us all her possessions went.

That is to say they did not find
A lawyer's Will of any kind.
Yet there was one in her own hand,
A Home for Ailing Cats she planned.
Well, you can understand my ire:
Promptly I put it in the fire.

In misery she chose to die,
Yet we will make her money fly.
And as we mourn for poor Aunt Jane
The thought alleviates our pain:
Perhaps her savings in the end
Gave her more joy than we who spend.

******

You've heard of Violet de Vere, strip-teaser of renown,
Whose sitting-base out-faired the face of any girl in town;
Well, she was haled before the Bench for breachin'
of the Peace,
Which signifies araisin' Cain, an' beatin' up the police.
So there she stood before the Court of ruddy
Judge McGraw
Whom folks called Old Necessity, because he knew
no law.
Aye, crackin' in a silken gown, an' sheddin' of a tear,
Ashine wi' gold an' precious stones sat Violet de Vere.
Old Judge McGraw looked dourly down an' stroked his
silver beard.

Says he: "Although the Sheriff's bruised, the lady
should be heared.
What can you say in your defence? We'll give you
a square deal."
"I jest forget," said Violet. "Maybe it was my heel.
I always want to kick the gong when I am feelin' gay;
It's most unfortunate, I guess, his face was in the way."
Then scratchin' of his snowy pow the Judge looked
down severe,
Where bright wi' paint like plaster saint sat Violet de Vere.

Says he: "I'm going to impose a twenty dollar fine."
Says Violet: "Your Honour, to your judgement I resign.
I realize I should not my agility reveal:
Next time I'll kick the Sheriff with my toe and
not my heel.
I'm grateful to the Court because I'm not put in the clink;
There's twenty plunks to pay my fine, but now I
come to think:
Judge, darlin', you've been owin' me five bucks for
near a year:
Take fifteen, there! We'll call it square," said Violet de Vere.

Following the war, Robert Service returned to France
where he continued to write. In his lifetime he published
16 volumes of poetry, six novels and three of books of non-
fiction. Not relying entirely on the pen, he also dabbled in
music and was involved in the writing of at least seven songs.

The Christmas Tree

In the dark and damp of the alley cold,
Lay the Christmas tree that hadn't been sold;
By a shopman dourly thrown outside;
With the ruck and rubble of Christmas-tide;
Trodden deep in the muck and mire,
Unworthy even to feed a fire...
So I stopped and salvaged that tarnished tree,
And this is the story it told to me:

"My Mother was Queen of the forest glade,
And proudly I prospered in her shade;
For she said to me: 'When I am dead,
You will be monarch in my stead,
And reign, as I, for a hundred years,
A tower of triumph amid your peers,
When I crash in storm I will yield you space;
Son, you will worthily take my place.'

"So I grew in grace like a happy child,
In the heart of the forest free and wild;
And the moss and the ferns were all about,
And the craintive mice crept in and out;
And a wood-dove swung on my highest twig,
And a chipmunk chattered: 'So big! So big!'
And a shy fawn nibbled a tender shoot,
And a rabbit nibbled under my root...
Oh, I was happy in rain and shine
As I thought of the destiny that was mine!
Then a man with an axe came cruising by
And I knew that my fate was to fall and die.

"With a hundred others he packed me tight,
And we drove to a magic city of light,
To an avenue lined with Christmas trees,
And I thought: maybe I'll be one of these,
Tinselled with silver and tricked with gold,
A lovely sight for a child to behold;
A-glitter with lights of every hue,
Ruby and emerald, orange and blue,
And kiddies dancing, with shrieks of glee -
One might fare worse than a Christmas tree.

"So they stood me up with a hundred more
In the blaze of a big department store;
But I thought of the forest dark and still,
And the dew and the snow and the heat and the chill,
And the soft chinook and the summer breeze,
And the dappled deer and the birds and the bees...
I was so homesick I wanted to cry,
But patient I waited for someone to buy.
And some said 'Too big,' and some 'Too small,'
And some passed on saying nothing at all.
Then a little boy cried: Ma, buy that one,'
But she shook her head: 'Too dear, my son."
So the evening came, when they closed the store,
And I was left on the littered floor,
A tree unwanted, despised, unsold,
Thrown out at last in the alley cold."

Then I said: "Don't sorrow; at least you'll be
A bright and beautiful New Year's tree,
All shimmer and glimmer and glow and gleam,
A radiant sight like a fairy dream.
For there is a little child I know,
Who lives in poverty, want and woe;
Who lies abed from morn to night,
And never has known an hour's delight..."

So I stood the tree at the foot of her bed:
"Santa's a little late," I said.
"Poor old chap! Snowbound on the way,
But he's here at last, so let's be gay."
Then she woke from sleep and she saw you there,
And her eyes were love and her lips were prayer.
And her thin little arms were stretched to you
With a yearning joy that they never knew.
She woke from the darkest dark to see
Like a heavenly vision, that Christmas Tree.

Her mother had despaired and feared the end,
But from that day on she began to mend,
To play, to sing, to laugh with glee...
Bless you, O little Christmas Tree!
You died, but your life was not in vain:
You helped a child to forget her pain,
And let hope live in our hearts again.

For all good friends who care to read,
here let me lyre my living creed

One: you may deem me Pacifist,
For I've no sympathy with strife.
Like hell I hate the iron fist,
And shun the battle-ground of life.
The hope of peace is dear to me,
And I to Christian faith belong,
Holding that breath should sacred be,
And War is always wrong.

Two: Universalist am I
And dream a world that's frontier free,
With common tongue and common tie,
Uncurst by nationality;
Where colour, creed and class are one,
And lowly folk are lifted high;
Where every breed beneath the sun
Is equal in God's eye.

Three: you may call me Naturist,
For green glade is my quiet quest;
The path of progress I have missed,
And shun the city's sore unrest.
A world that's super-civilized
Is one of worry, want and woe;
In leafy lore let me be wised
And back to Nature go.

Well, though you may but half agree,
Behold my trusty Trinity

Service passed away at his home in Lancieux, France on September 11, 1958, age 84. His wife, Germaine, 13 years younger than her husband, survived him by 31 years and died aged 102 in December of 1989 in Monte Carlo. He died a rich artist, mostly famous as a writer of poetry. Take that you critics! Shortly before leaving his eventful and fruitful life he wrote –

I guess this is the final score:
Alas! I now shall write no more,
Though sad's my mood;
Since I've been 60 years a bard,
I must admit it's rather hard
To quit for good.

For three-score years I've roped in rhyme,
Till weary of the worn-out chime
I've sought for new;
But I've decided in the end,
With thirty-thousand couplets penned,
The old must do.
So let this be the last of me;
No more my personality
I'll plant in verse;
Within a year I may be dead,
Then my books are no more read,
I'm none the worse.

Far better scribes than I have gone
The way to bleak oblivion
With none to sigh;

Ah, well! My writing's been such fun,
And now my job of work is done,
Dear friends, who've let me have my run,
Good-bye – good-bye

Exit– Blackout

ENCORE

Enter to Tight Spot

A bunch of the boys were whooping it up
in the Malamute saloon;
The kid that handles the music-box
was hitting a rag-time tune;
Back of the bar, in a solo game,
sat Dangerous Dan McGrew,
And watching his luck was his light-o'-love,
the lady that's known as Lou.

When out of the night, which was fifty below,
and into the din and glare,
There stumbled a miner fresh from the creeks,
dog-dirty, and loaded for bear.
He looked like a man with a foot in the grave
and scarcely the strength of a louse,
Yet he tilted a poke of dust on the bar,
and he called for drinks for the house.

There was none could place the stranger's face,
though we searched ourselves for a clue;
But we drank his health, and the last to drink
was Dangerous Dan McGrew.

There's men that somehow just grip your eyes,
and hold them hard like a spell;
And such was he, and he looked to me like
a man who had lived in hell;
With a face most hair, and the dreary stare
of a dog whose day is done,
As he watered the green stuff in his glass,
and the drops fell one by one.

Then I got to figgering who he was,
and wondering what he'd do,
And I turned my head — and there watching him
was the lady that's known as Lou.

His eyes went rubbering round the room,
and he seemed in a kind of daze,
Till at last that old piano fell in the way
of his wandering gaze.
The rag-time kid was having a drink;
there was no one else on the stool,
So the stranger stumbles across the room,
and flops down there like a fool.

In a buckskin shirt that was glazed with dirt
he sat, and I saw him sway,
Then he clutched the keys with his talon hands
my God! but that man could play.

Were you ever out in the Great Alone,
when the moon was awful clear,
And the icy mountains hemmed you in
with a silence you most could hear;
With only the howl of a timber wolf,
and you camped there in the cold,
A half-dead thing in a stark, dead world,
clean mad for the muck called gold;

While high overhead, green, yellow, and red,
the North Lights swept in bars?
Then you've a hunch what the music meant
hunger and night and the stars.

And hunger not of the belly kind,
that's banished with bacon and beans,
But the gnawing hunger of lonely men
for a home and all that it means;
For a fireside far from the cares that are,
four walls and a roof above;
But oh! so cramful of cosy joy,
and crowded with a woman's love

A woman dearer than all the world,
and true as Heaven is true
(God! how ghastly she looks through her rouge,
the lady that's known as Lou.)

Then on a sudden the music changed,
so soft that you scarce could hear;
But you felt that your life had been looted clean
of all that it once held dear;
That someone had stolen the woman you loved;
that her love was a devil's lie;
That your guts were gone, and the best for you
was to crawl away and die.

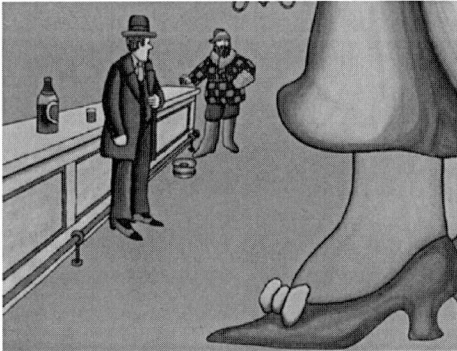

'Twas the crowning cry of a heart's despair,
and it thrilled you through and through
"I guess I'll make it a spread misere,"
said Dangerous Dan McGrew.

The music almost dies away
then it burst like a pent-up flood;
And it seemed to say, "Repay, repay,"
and my eyes were blind with blood.
The thought came back of an ancient wrong,
and it stung like a frozen lash,
And the lust awoke to kill, to kill
then the music stopped with a crash,
And the stranger turned, and his eyes
they burned in a most peculiar way;

In a buckskin shirt that was glazed with dirt
he sat, and I saw him sway;
Then his lips went in in a kind of grin,
and he spoke, and his voice was calm,
And "Boys," says he, "you don't know me,
and none of you care a damn;
But I want to state, and my words are straight,
and I'll bet my poke they're true,
That one of you is a hound of hell
and that one is Dan McGrew."

Then I ducked my head and the lights went out,
and two guns blazed in the dark;
And a woman screamed, and the lights went up,
and two men lay stiff and stark.
Pitched on his head, and pumped full of lead,
was Dangerous Dan McGrew,
While the man from the creeks lay clutched
to the breast of the lady that's known as Lou.

These are the simple facts of the case,
and I guess I ought to know.
They say that the stranger was crazed with "hooch,"
and I'm not denying it's so.
I'm not so wise as the lawyer guys,
but strictly between us two
The woman that kissed him
and pinched his poke
was the lady that's known as Lou.

Works by Robert Service

Poetry

- "Carry On!" (date missing)
- *Songs of a Sourdough* (1907)
  - o *[U.S. as The Spell of the Yukon and Other Verses]*
- *Ballads of a Cheechako* (1909)
- *Rhymes of a Rolling Stone* (1912)
- *Songs of the Yukon* (1913)
- *Rhymes of a Red-Cross Man* (1916)
- *Ballads of a Bohemian* (1921)
- *Twenty Bath-Tub Ballads* (1939)
- *Bar-Room Ballads* (1940)
- *Songs of a Sun-Lover. A Book of Light Verse* (1949)
- *Rhymes of a Roughneck. A Book of Verse* (1950)
- *Lyrics of a Lowbrow. A Book of Verse* (1951)
- *Rhymes of a Rebel. A Book of Verse* (1952)
- *Songs for my Supper* (1953)
- *Carols of an Old Codger* (1955)
- *Rhymes for My Rags* (1956)

Fiction

- *The Trail of Ninety-Eight, A Northland Romance* (1909)
- *The Pretender. A story of the Latin quarter* (1914)
- *The Poisoned Paradise: A Romance of Monte Carlo* (1922)
- *The Roughneck, A Tale of Tahiti* (1923)
- *The Master of the Microbe: A Fantastic Romance* (1926)
- *The House of Fear, A Novel* (1927)

Non-fiction

- *Why Not Grow Young? or Living for Longevity* (1928)
- *Ploughman of the Moon, An Adventure Into Memory* (1945) – autobiography
- *Harper of Heaven. A Record of Radiant Living* (1948) – autobiography

Music

- *Twenty Bath-Tub Ballads* (1939)
- *Tripe and Trotters* (words and music, 1939)
- *The Amorous* (Square words and music, 1939)
- *If you can't be Good be Careful* (words and music, 1939)
- *My old School Tie* (words and music, 1939)
- *Facility words* (words by Robert W. Service & Music by Leslie T. Cochran, G. Ricordi & C° Ltd London)
- *Unforgotten* (words by Robert W. Service & Music by Fredrick Sixten, 2012) published by Gehrmans Musikförlag, Stockholm, Sweden

First Line Identifies Poem Title (Italics)

Other titles by Clint Ward

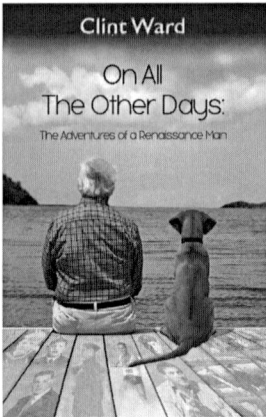

Clint Ward
On All The Other Days:
The Adventures of a Renaissance Man

A memoir of the multi dimensional renaissance journey of author Clint Ward. It is a rare glimpse 'behind the curtain' of a life well lived, interwoven with epic proportions of high flying adventure sportsmanship and world travel. Revel in the details of this literary and photographic odyssey.

Clint's research on women pilots during the Second World War in England led to his writing a play called *Spitfire Dance* which was about the Air Transport Auxiliary and their women pilots. The play opened in the fall of 2014 at Canada's War Museum in Ottawa.

Spitfire Dance
a Play of Remembrance
by Clint Ward

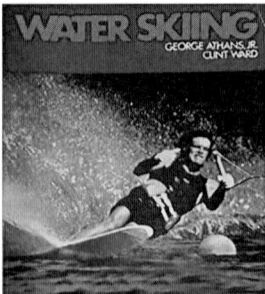

WATER SKIING
GEORGE ATHANS JR.
CLINT WARD

Jointly written with George Athans. Contents include: How it all began, Anyone can learn to Water Ski, Equipment, Boat Driving, Slalom Skiing, Figure Skiing, Jumping, World Water Ski Union Member Countries, World Water Ski Championships.

Ordering info at www.clintward.ca